Change Is For the Brave

-

Joseph Barlow

A Publication of
JBM

Special thanks to:

Sarah Barlow - Cover and layout design
Timothy Aikenhead - Editorial guidance
Janet Peluso - Editorial and layout guidance

ISBN: 978-0-9971678-8-7

www.josephbarlow.com

To my dearest friend, H.S.,
Who is the true master of Change!

Introduction

Deep waters ahead, slow reading required.

Take your time. We're not in a hurry.
This journey will be so rewarding.

I believe
change is possible
and you believe
change is necessary.

Affecting change in our lives can be so elusive! We grasp for it, but it can just slip away from us when we continue in our same patterns of behavior.

Why? Is there a key? We're going to have to dive deep into our hearts.

Through sayings, stories, questions, and explanations, let's start a journey together into this often elusive but extremely powerful solution called CHANGE!

Joe

Part 1

Change Is for The Brave

Change starts with
seeing that
where you are
is not
where you want to be.

It's time to move!

Change begins
when you see
correction is needed
in your life,
and you are willing
to adopt new ways.

New desires are
calling you
to give up
your old,
failed routines.

It's time to dig
new furrows,
the old ones
are easier to follow
but they're taking you
down the wrong road.

In making
lasting change,
your WILL shall be
constantly challenged
until new habits
are formed.

Change is
re-aligning
your beliefs,
actions,
practices,
and habits
to a truth
that is new to you.

When discipline leads
to a new habit
your desires
begin to line up with
a new way and you
have arrived at a
station in life –
one where you're not
hurting yourself with
your own actions.

Status quo is where
the furrows are deep,
the habits are set,
you don't fight you
just flow –
just be sure you're
flowing in
the direction
you want to go.

Are you on the bus
that takes you to your
intended destination?

Habits are moving
you somewhere.

Habits are programs
in you that run
continually
until you
break
or replace them.

Habits are extraordinarily helpful!

With habits we've
decided a pathway
and programmed that
into our whole being:
our thoughts,
tendencies, leanings,
desires, even
muscle-memory all
flow in the same
direction.

There’s
very little stress
in continuing
wholeheartedly
in a habit.

Changing your
subconscious mind
is indeed
a process –
it is the place in you
where all habits
dwell.

Negative habits are set because you continued in them when in fact you should have resisted.

Right habits
lead to an end
that you love.

Establishing right habits comes from knowing where you want to go and who you want to be.

Habits are in place because you put them there.

How blessed we are
to have a system
where our desires are
fulfilled by our habits
continuing to propel
us forward to where
we want to go!

Continuous
incremental change
is the habit's way.

Falling out of love
with old ways –

Seeing negative habits
as enemies will help
you leave them.

Habits bring
continuous
incremental change –
for better, for worse,
for richer, for poorer.

Who knows?
You might need to
divorce some of your
habits.

Habits provide programs that rise from within you automatically running your schedule.

Unlocking the intricate system of habit is the key to changing your destiny.

Habits
reduce
the conscious
decisions
to be made,
which relieves much
stress!

Habits that degrade your life are not your friends.

Take cover!

You are entering a
war zone!

Wage the war well.

Negative habits are enemies that can be defeated.

Know your enemies and destroy them.

Seize the victory!

Resolve is required,
but stress comes when
two desires within
you clash.

Now a decision must
be made, and you
can't fight on both
sides.

Decisions…
Deciding…

There is a root word in there that means "to cut," like incision or excision.

Deciding to cut something from your life is not easy…

But, new paths and
horizons
lie beyond the reach
of the indecision
that binds you.

Your mind…
Your body…
Your heart…

All the members of who you are, want to work together.

Let them unite in a single direction.

Deciding between two
desires could mean
the death of one and
the life of the other,
but not deciding could
mean the death of
both.

Trust your gut!
Make a cut.
Choose you must,
or all will bust.

Indecision
is your enemy.

Be bold!

CHOOSE!

If clarity
of desire
eludes you…

so will
progress.

Desire what's best.
Desire it deeply.
Let that desire burn
within you and
change the core of
who you are.

Not desiring…

is unhealthy for you.

Desires polarize your whole being, bringing amazing order.

Like when you have a crush on someone, everything in you wants to serve that desire.

There is beauty in singleness of purpose.

Desires align your
whole person.

They draw all the
energies from every
part of you to serve
the one desire.

Healthy alignment.

Unity of purpose –

Your whole self prefers to serve one desire rather than endure the stress of not knowing which desire to serve.

Amazing power and potential are released when your whole self comes into alignment with one purpose.

Deeply held beliefs
go unchallenged
within you.

You allow no
contenders.

Like your immune
system fighting
infection, all contrary
beliefs will be
resisted.

Every word you hear
must obey your
deepest beliefs or
you'll reject them.

Contrary voices will
eventually be silenced
in your world.

You'll make sure of it.

Any belief within you
that has no action
attached to it,
may need to be
reconsidered.

You don't believe it
enough to do what
may be required.

There comes a time when you just have to get up off the couch and go do what you believe.

The future is passing
through a portal to
become the past;
the portal is called…

"Now"

One purpose at a time
please.

Judging your current
condition...

if you like it then
leave it alone...

if not…

are you willing to
change?

Are You Ready?

You can do this!

Change is
for the BRAVE!

Part 2

Let’s Talk About Change

Friends,

Wisdom has been too elusive these days. Where can you find it? Knowledge is easy. There's plenty of that. But wisdom is knowing what to do with the knowledge you have. So where do we find wisdom?

An old proverb says:

**"To be wise,
walk with the wise."**

I don't want to claim to be wise – that would be foolish, but if you find any wisdom in these sayings, then walk with me through these pages.

Enjoy,

Joe

One Life Changed

Years ago, a young mother called to tell me that her husband, a friend of mine, was in jail.

I said, "What happened?"

She said, "I put him there."

She put him in jail for child neglect as he had gone down the street to buy a case of beer while the children were at home alone and she was away. I knew on the inside of me that I should go bail him out and take him into our home.

To other's, me proposing to my family to have a young, very muscular black man with a felony and a gang background to live with us may have sounded crazy. Maybe not the wisest move for a father. But my wife, Nancy, was in 100% agreement, as were my children. We all loved him and wanted to see his life turned around.

So, I visited him at the county jail, and we talked through the visitor's window. I shared my list of rules and requirements with him. If he was willing to follow them, I would bail him out.

He agreed. I bailed him out, brought him home and my family welcomed him with open arms.

He did great. He would do the reading assignments I gave him. He would eat with the family. He would keep his area clean. He would go jogging with my wife. He would do work around the house to pay off his bail.

When my older children were going into the city to do photo shoots he would ask to go along. When they got home, he said, "I've never been in a situation where a group of kids went out to have fun without committing a crime." Wow!

Our culture was different. Our family was different. Our family was the recipe for what he needed at that time. He was wonderful to have around the house. We all loved him dearly. He kept his word and followed my requirements.

Something was changing in him.

Something was changing him.

He was being transformed.

After three months his marriage was reconciled, and he went home to be with his wife and children.

After several more months his wife called me to say, “I thought I should call you and give you a piece of my mind.”
I said, “Oh yeah!?”

She said, “Since he returned home, the way he treats me is totally different. The way he treats our children is totally different. The way he treats my parents, and his parents is totally different.” She said, “I just wanted you to know that. Thank you.”

What a privilege to be a part of such an exciting transformation. I'm so glad our family was able to be a catalyst of such a beautiful change. We were an environment that catapulted this young man forward in ways that nothing else could.

This change came about because there was life-on-life. One life was changed by another. Better than that, one life was changed by a community that held to certain standards and was strong enough within itself to not be negatively influenced from without.

This was among the most rapid life changes I've seen.

Community is formative,
family is transformative.

When my friend joined our family for those three months, he was joining a community. Aside from my written requirements, there was silent influence upon him to conform to the norms and standards we lived by.

He observed our way of life; the happiness in our children, our marriage, our faith community. He developed an appetite for what we had. He allowed himself to be taken in by it. To be enveloped by it. To be transformed by it.

Cultural environment is transformative.
Herein lies the power of family.

Where a culture dwells in unity, when they think in generally the same direction, acting according to an agreed upon moral standard, life is much simpler. Cultural unity silently demands conformity. This can be wonderful when the make-up of the society is good. It can be devastating when it is bad.

In our family, we have our standards. We have our ways. We've done our best to create an atmosphere of love where each child can grow and develop, where they can discover who they are. Where they are surrounded with family love and support.

Get Changed or Be the Change

Since we've learned that cultural environment is transformative to those who live within it, you either need to…

1. Lead by displaying the character and nature that you want the culture to conform to or you need to…
2. Join a culture that already is made up of people you need to become like.

Let me re-write that:

1. Lead and get your culture to conform to you or
2. Join a culture that you need to conform to

One more time:

1. Lead or
2. Conform

The environment you're in is either changing you or conforming to you.

It is conforming you or conforming to you!

Leadership is necessary for the formation of culture.

Families follow their leader. If you are a leader, then be a leader.

Leadership is you setting the standard.

It leads others in the culture of your house, organization, or group. That culture is formative. It demands others align with it.

People will change themselves to align with a standard they love or respect.
Being out of tune with your culture causes sufficient discomfort to affect change.

Either get into the culture that embodies what you desire to become or become what you are supposed to be and let your example change and lead your culture. Then others may conform to your standard as you hopefully affect and elevate your culture.

Pick Your Teachers

My dad told me right at the end of 8th grade, "If you find a teacher that you like, take classes from them, even if you're not interested in the topic – you learn from the individual." This was an important lesson as I entered high school and had the opportunity to choose my own classes.

You are naturally attracted to leaders. Something on the inside of you is already in tune with what's coming from them. That's why you want to follow them.

Be on guard, some leaders are dark, and some are light. You must be careful that your own heart is right, or light, or you could end up multiplying darkness by following someone who has darkness on the inside of them.

Follow leaders who are going where you know you are supposed to go. Your best internal convictions are most often right. Seek the right. Seek the light!

Running

I used to jog with my sister in the mornings during summer vacation when I was maybe 10. I've run at different times in my life.

We've had a treadmill and have put some effort into our exercise routine. But they had a running club at our old church, and I was content to just let them run!

"Have a good time. I'll watch!" Ha-ha!

But then I became friends with the leader of the club. His influence started affecting me. He led over 1,000 people across the finish line at the Chicago Marathon.

Under his tutelage, even sedentary people would complete the marathon.

He is a Champion Maker!

Once you start hanging around with good people, they will affect you positively. I never had a desire to run a marathon, but I did have a desire to run more than 10 miles. I had never done that.

Somehow, he convinced me to join the running club. My two oldest kids wanted to join as well. Sarah was 16 and Andrew, 14.

We started in January going to all the classes they held. In the Spring it was time to go down and run on the Chicago lakeshore on Saturday mornings, at or before sunrise.

Our first run was one mile. The next week, two miles. Oh boy! This was coming fast. You learn so much more when you get out and practice what you've been studying!

My kids did great, but once we got to 14 miles my knees said, "Sorry, no more!"

The day we ran 14 miles, I only ran about 8, walked about two or three miles then limped the rest of the way back!

I was satisfied, I accomplished my goal. But this opened the door for my son to run the Chicago Marathon in October at age 15. (The minimum age is 16, but we got an exception.) Andrew and Sarah both finished the race. I was so proud of them.

We started with the club in January and by October the two of them ran the marathon. We were deeply impacted and transformed by the community that we chose to join.

Running a marathon is no small undertaking. Mental and physical transformation are essential for such a feat. The community we joined helped to bring about that transformation.

There are all kinds of groups you could join: church small groups, study groups, masterminds, gym classes, schools, even family gatherings.

What kind of group is doing what is most in line with the dreams of your heart?

Each of these groups bear standards that expect conformity. Use this to your advantage. Join a group, a family or a culture that is going in the direction you want to go.

Create or form a tribe, culture, society, or group that conforms to a cultural recipe that you see is needful.

Who you become is determined by what you desire and are willing to do.

Based on what you see in your life and in your world:

- Is it time to start…

  A new group?

  A new tribe?

  A new society?
- Are you the leader?
- Are you strong enough in those winning traits that you could lead by embodying those characteristics?
- Could you lead such a culture?
- Are you strong enough?
- Do you need strengthening?
- Where are you going to get that strength?

My Life Changed When…

As we are in pursuit of how to change, let us consider some examples. Looking at my own life here are some examples of when the trajectory of my life took a turn for the better. Some of them may seem simple but look for the cause and the effect.

A New Guitar

My life changed when my dad bought me a guitar, I gained a new focus. I had a new toy and a new expression. Now I had something that would take this river of musical creativity on the inside of me and give it a place to flow. I started playing guitar all the time. My mom called my guitar an extra appendage. It became part of who I am.

A New Stereo

My life changed again when my brother bought me a record player with AM/FM and cassette for Christmas when I was 12. Having the right equipment to match your talents makes all the difference in the world.

At the same time my sister bought me an album by Todd Rundgren, A Wizard - A True Star. My world opened up. My dreams of musicianship and record production were seeded during this time. If Todd could play all the instruments on his album, I wanted to shoot for that!

Having my guitar along with a record player with AM/FM radio and a cassette player…I was set! I could learn anything I wanted. I learned so much. The hours I spent with my guitar and that equipment numbered in the thousands.

Without the right equipment you can be severely handicapped, not able to do what you could do if you just had the right equipment.

A New Songbook

My life changed at 13 when I bought a book of music for an album that I liked. It had a piano song in there. I went to my mom and asked her. "How do you read music?"
She said,

"Do you see that dot there with a line
through it right in the middle?
That is middle C."
She said, "The space above it is D.
The line above that is E.
The space below C is B.
The line below that is A."

I said, "It just goes on from there?"
She said, "Yeah."
I said, "Is that it?"
She said, "Well, you have to know sharps and flats."

She explained that and she showed me the corresponding keys on the piano and I was off and running. I started playing piano every day, learning, and memorizing one measure a day. This took hours of my focus and energy.

Again, I was a completely new person because this opportunity to play the piano brought new expression to my life. There was a pathway through which my creativity could flow. I grew rapidly.

Switching Teachers

My life changed again the day my brother taught me how to learn a song off the record player. Up until this point, I was learning guitar from my older brothers and sisters. I was so hungry to learn that I took in everything they could teach me. There's an old saying that says:

You can't go beyond your teachers.

You can be like them, but you can never exceed them.

Well, my siblings were my teachers, so I couldn't exceed them. But the day Vince taught me to learn off the record player, he was no longer my teacher. From then on the record player was my teacher. I exceeded my siblings by switching teachers.

Learning A New Skill

My life changed when I learned data normalization. Now stick with me! There is so much data in this world, and keeping track of it all is no small task. When I found out that there was a method and a system by which we could organize all of the data that we are trying to keep track of, it made a huge difference.

I studied data normalization at my job. In trying to bring order to my telemarketing department and all the data we had to manage; I was taking them from a manual paper lead system to a completely computerized sales system.

Learning data normalization profoundly impacted the way that I think. It gave me a new algorithm through which my thoughts could flow.

A New Friend

My life changed again the day that I first met my friend Dave back in my freshman year of college. He is high energy and vision driven. He is positive and supportive. He is full of wisdom, and we just seemed to click. Even later in life when we hadn't seen each other for 10 years, then sat down for dinner, it was just like we had never been apart.

My life changed from this because I had a different level of confidence and effectiveness. I knew that I had a friend I could talk to and gain support and wisdom from. His friendship has proven valuable so many times through all these years.

A New Perspective

My life changed when I had a spiritual conversion experience. At age 11, I heard my brother talking to my Dad. Their conversation lasted three hours. I sat and consumed the whole thing, listening. The thoughts expressed in that conversation became my new reality.

All of life made sense now.

When a new paradigm comes into position on the inside of you and you are in tune with it, it changes you.

A New Way to Communicate

My life changed again when I saw a friend stick her tongue out at our two-day old son, he responded by sticking his tongue out at her. He was only two days old! She said this is the only thing they can do to respond to you.

I realized that I now had a way of communicating even with infants.

From then on, I knew I could communicate with babies and little children.

It's fun in restaurants and grocery stores when you catch the glance of a child or infant and it feels right, stick your tongue out at them, they immediately focus on responding to you.

There've even been times when a child was a little out of control and making lots of noise when I would do this, and they stop making noise and start focusing on sticking their tongue out at me.

Like shaking a hand with an adult, this little exchange can be the beginning of a relationship with a child before they learn to speak.

I now had a new ingredient for our recipe in communicating with children and for parenting.

A New Truth

We've had great success in our parenting, but when we got this key, it put everything else in perspective. Our key to parenting is this:

If you can obtain
and maintain
an open-heart relationship
with your child,
you will never lose them.

I feel the responsibility to win the hearts of my children. So, I started young when I could connect with them by sticking my tongue out at them. I want to use creative means to connect with them towards building a great relationship. This can start quite early.

I do the same now with my grandchildren. We are having a wonderful time. Some of them can't even talk yet, but we still have a grand time. My life was changed by this knowledge and the application of it.

A New Focus

My life changed the day my father told me I was selfish for getting nervous in front of the class.

I was presenting a project in 5th grade and couldn't control my quivering lip. He said I was more concerned about myself than the people I was supposed to be helping.

This change of focus has enabled me to speak in front of thousands and literally millions without being nervous.

The energy is supposed to be flowing from me to them during a presentation. If I get too concerned with the flow of energy from them to me it confuses and adds to the nerves.

Breaking Up

My life changed again in college when I was dating a girl and realized she was not to be my wife. I didn't want to continue investing in our relationship since it was only going to end.

Once I acted on that internal conviction, I felt like I was walking on air. I felt so relieved. It really had nothing to do with her. It had to do with me making a decision about my future and sticking with it.

That break up allowed me to align with my destiny with my wife, Nancy.

A New Partner

My life changed when I married Nancy. I finally found someone who loved God more than I did! I allowed my whole life to align with our destiny as a couple.

We don't necessarily agree on every detail, but we love each other and are committed to one another. We have seen so much fruit come from our alignment. We have now been married for several decades and have seven children and many grandchildren. We are so blessed!

I often say, if it hadn't been for Nancy, I would still be living in a one-bedroom apartment, playing my guitar, eating macaroni and cheese, and sometimes putting ham in it! But my life has become so much more because of our marriage.

A Dangerous Prayer

My life changed the day I prayed one of those dangerous prayers. That's a prayer that you naively pray with all good intentions, but the answer can be quite painful when it arrives.

I had heard a scripture that said, "Guard your heart, because out of it flow the boundaries of your life."

I looked at the boundaries of my life and I didn't like what I was seeing. My music was still relatively unknown in the world, I couldn't make progress with my weight loss, the church I was leading hadn't been growing and I knew that I was the problem.

Then I asked the Lord to "Do what you need to do in me to move the boundaries of my heart." It seems He delighted to answer the prayer, but the answer was not the easiest thing to receive.

I had an assistant working for me who God started using to get at the core issues of my heart. These issues were great hindrances to me, they were in fact the boundaries of my life; stopping all the answers I really wanted.

In our daily conversations as we worked together, she would challenge me on things. I had told her early on in her employment that "if I can't share my heart with you completely then you're not the right person to be working with me."

Well, she was up for the challenge. It was important for me, in the way I process things, to have someone to process them with. She was ideal for that. But because I was opening my heart to her (not in any romantic way) my heart was exposed in a way that God could answer that naive prayer to ‘move the boundaries of my heart’. She had access to those boundaries, and she gladly challenged their existence.

Her questions and challenges to me were so penetrating and challenging that I could truly feel the boundaries of my heart being moved. That is no small feat. It was painful at times. But her words were true and golden.

I didn’t always perceive her words as golden. She had actually confessed to a friend that she thought this was the first job she would ever get fired from. She said, “One day I might push him too far.”

Well, one day she did.

I thought, “That’s enough. I don’t need this woman pushing me around.” On the way home from work I had decided to fire her, but when I got home, I sat on the side of my bed and opened my Bible. It came right open to the passage where Jesus says, “Put your sword away! Shall I not drink the cup that my Father has ordained for me to drink?" I thought, "Uh oh! I'm about to get corrected!"

Then the Lord spoke to me and said, **"Son, it's me. There are still areas of your heart that are blocking my love."** I knew from that point God was working through her to answer my prayer. I changed my perspective about her work and went back to work the next day for more of the same.

Her voice has been an important one in my life. Even years after she left, I would still call her back and hire her to coach me through certain seasons. Her words truly have been golden.

When real change is happening on the inside of us, it most likely will get to an uncomfortable place where you don't want to continue.

But don't quit! Change in all of us is so important. It's worth the effort to go through the process.

A New Coach

My life changed when I hired a coach to help me lose weight.

Because I spent so much money on the program, I wanted to make sure that it was a wise investment. So, I aligned myself completely with his program. I was very diligent. I was accountable to him for everything I ate. The result was I lost 30 pounds in six months. That was great!

Joe, so have you been able to keep all the weight off that you lost?

Actually, no.

I gained some back, but not all of it. So, it wasn't the full change I wanted. True change would be demonstrated by keeping the weight off.

The coaching program educated me, probably saved my life, gave me an opportunity to change.

So why didn't it stick?

When I was coached, I was submitting to a controlled environment. Maybe I then started submitting to the less controlled environment of our family's eating habits.

Maybe I was good at submitting to the environment around me.

Diets often fail for lack of practical and moral support.

Coaching was great for me. I made great progress. I had the support and resolve that I needed.

Some people come into your life naturally, others you must pay to be there. You must decide what you need. Put it in place.

I needed the influence, knowledge, and wisdom in my life to rescue me from being overweight.

But did real change happen?

To my physical body it did. To my internal psyche, my habits, and my will, it may not have happened completely.

With my weight loss program what we saw was the yielding to influence. I needed the influence, so I paid to have that influence in my life.

“So, do we need to hire or install influence until real change happens? How come the coaching program for weight loss didn’t truly change you?”

“If you’re not able to keep the weight off without a coach, have you truly changed or just been yielding to influence, paid or free?”

I want to be changed. I know more now than I did before the coaching program. But some internal systems that were in place that caused weight gain are still in place.

Do I know how to lose weight?

Yes.

Do I have the willpower to do it?

Seems debatable. I have more work to do.

Valid change is proven by the result.

Can I lose weight without the influence of a coach?

Not until change happens in the deeper parts of me.

How will you affect the change you need? Where will it come from?

If influence upon you to follow the standard doesn't change you, then we need to dig deeper. There must be a way to change the core beliefs, motivations, drivers, and habits that steer someone's daily actions.

There are several factors that influence whether or not lasting change happens in you. Let's explore…

Changing Your Set-Point

When a pilot sets his airplane to autopilot, he puts the altitude at a certain level. Let's call it a set-point. If he sets the altitude to 30,000 ft. that airplane will continue to correct and stay at 30,000 ft. If, while the autopilot is engaged, he pushes the stick down to bring the airplane down to 28,000 ft. then it will stay at 28,000 ft. until he lets his hand off the stick. The autopilot kicks back in and returns the plane to 30,000 ft. If he pulls back on the stick and brings the plane up to 32,000 ft. letting go returns it to 30,000 ft. because of its set-point.

The question is do you have a set-point that needs to change?

Do you have a place within you that is a place of comfort where that's where you want to be? Your subconscious mind keeps bringing you back to your set-point. If that's the case, then we must learn how to change our set-point.

When we can see someone else do something, it's easier for us to see ourselves doing it.

After Roger Bannister broke the 4-minute mile in 1954, many other runners were able to break the 4-minute mile. They could see themselves doing it because they could see Roger Bannister doing it.

Having a role model that goes ahead of you is a great blessing. You watch what they do, you imitate them, you conform your actions to what you see them doing.

But what if you are the pioneer? What if there is no role model for you? Well, we have been designed with an imagination.

That imagination has the capability of creating a picture of a role model for you to follow. You can create a scene in your imagination where you are the hero and as the hero you go in and accomplish some great feat that you know you are supposed to do. For me it might be bringing my weight down to a new normal. If I spend time in that imagination making it as real as I am able, if I let myself experience the emotions and whatever tactile feelings I can experience from that imagination, and if I see myself establishing a new set-point in my imagination, it can in fact be changed.

This is only the beginning of a discussion about personal change, there is so much more to be said and learned and so much more to be experimented and researched.

Close your eyes and do the meditation yourself. Do the prayer or speaking to yourself, writing things down and making quality determinant decisions to affect your personal internal setpoint regarding any matter. Do the work. The answers are waiting for you.

Motivation

Joe, why don’t you just decide to lose weight? You know it's the right thing to do. You know it's healthier. You know it's more attractive. What is stopping you from deciding, getting with the program, aligning yourself and doing the right things?

Everyone is different to some degree. The recipe that created each of us is different from the next person. We are very individual. And as I like to say,

**“You are unique!
Just like everyone else!”**

Haha!

What motivates one person does nothing for the next.

We are equipped with what we’ve been given in life. But too many don’t know how to use what they’ve been given.

It's like each one of us has been dealt a hand of cards, we must decide how we are going to use them. Many of us have no idea how to use the cards we've been dealt.

That motivates me!

I have compassion for those who don't know what to do! I love teaching people what to do with what they've been dealt.

But if you said, "Lose weight Joe, it'll make you look more handsome."
That doesn't grab me.
Maybe a little. Very little.

If you said, "Lose weight Joe, it'll elongate your life. You'll get to see your grandkids grow up."
Now that motivates me.

Or if God himself spoke to me and said,
"Do it!
Lose weight now."
I would have zero hindrance to going

full-force into a weight-loss program.
I would be highly motivated.

Other people might be motivated by money, "Hey friend, if you lose 40 lbs. within a year, I'll give you $1,000. But if you lose it in nine months, I'll give you $1,500."

Different people reading this may find that one of these examples motivates them more than others.

Knowing what motivates you is keenly important. What feeds you? What gets you to move? What motivates you to action?

Increase Desire

Desires are essential.
It is what you really want.

If my wife were to invite me to get up off the couch to help her with the dishes, I'm not going to be very excited. I may be kind of slow getting up. I may even be searching for excuses to distract myself from having to get up and help with the dishes.

Why? Because I don't really want to!

Do you love your wife? Yes!

Do you want to see her happy? 100%

Now will you get up? Sure.

What if Nancy said, "Joe, I need to walk the dog, could you serve us both some ice cream so we could enjoy it together?" Getting myself up off the couch for that is very easy. There's no resistance.
Why?
You know why!

Sometimes we don't desire things enough.

Sometimes we get used to being disappointed, so we toughen ourselves up and get used to not getting what we want.

We get in the habit of suppressing our desires to the point that we stop desiring.

So, in searching for our motivations, you may find a landscape filled with broken dreams, dissatisfactions and forgotten desires. But it may be time for you to revisit one simple question:

"What do you want?"

Granted, this is not necessarily an easy question to answer. There can be a lot of chaff blocking the way from you being able to find the answer. But sit with it.

What do you want?

What would make you happy?

What dream should you revisit?

If you find the answer to those questions, congratulations! That's an accomplishment all by itself. But let me encourage you to take the next step.

Whatever it is that you want,
try this:

Desire it more.

Huh?

Yes. Desire it more.

How much do you want that thing?

If you were to gauge, on a scale from 1-10.
Are you a 6? A 4?

A few minutes ago, that desire was so suppressed in you that your desire level could have been considered a zero.

What is it now?

Let me encourage you: desire it more!

How?

If your desired level is a 6, then turn it up to a 7.

Imagine yourself turning the dial and resetting it at 7.

OK, that didn't work for me.

So, take that thing you desire and begin to see it fulfilled.

See it coming to pass in your life.

See yourself owning it or having accomplished it.

Now smile.

Be glad that you accomplished it or acquired it, even if just in your own imagination.

Another way to increase your desire is to describe out loud the emotions you will feel when it is accomplished or acquired.

Now borrow those emotions from your future. Feel those emotions now. Even if you can only do it partially, it's still a win.

If you do this, you are increasing your desire.

If you are successful in this little exercise, your motivation for action toward your desire will change.

Simply desire your desires.

Do it more actively.

Do it more intentionally.

As you desire something more you are moving yourself toward the place of action.

Discipline

Where desire is weak discipline must win the day!

Sit with that saying for a few moments.

Discipline is not required for you to eat ice cream.

It's the things you don’t want to do that require discipline.

But if you have a higher-level desire with a goal attached to it, that desire is strong enough for you to set a goal. That desire demands a certain regimen, a list of activities or practices to get you to your goal.

Disciplines are the list of activities that need to be programmed into our daily lives. If these are executed continuously, they lead us to the **win**!

I was disciplined while under the influence of my weight-loss coach and coaching program.

Habit

The daily disciplines however never became habitual.

Habit is where your actions are no longer initiated by your intellect and your will, but they come from your subconscious mind.

Transforming disciplines to habits is where the gold is.

Disciplines mostly come from the mind.
Habits come from the heart.

Disciplines mostly come from the mind.
They are our effort to bring change.
Habits come from the heart, as they have been programmed into our subconscious.

Discipline is needed when true change hasn't happened yet.

But habit is after true change has happened. You do the activity of the discipline, it doesn't feel like work to you, it's just something you do because that is who you are.

Habits show who you are.

Discipline is for becoming who you want to be.

Here's an interesting question to ponder:

How is getting a discipline to become a habit like falling asleep?

The process of falling asleep is where you lose consciousness. Your focus gets turned off. Once your focus is turned off you've entered another realm. Consciousness is turned off, but your brain doesn't shut off. Another portion of your brain takes over.

When I want a discipline to become a habit, I consciously repeat the discipline over and again. I want to develop muscle memory. I want it to be ingrained into my reactionary system.

For the discipline to become a habit, in a sense, I must fall asleep to it. So, I lose conscious control of the discipline. If my reactionary system still produces the same actions, then it has become a habit. It is written deeper inside of me than just in my intellect and cognitive thinking. It is a program within me that runs automatically.

I am in effect asleep to the discipline because I now have a habit that I can do subconsciously.

How Do You Change Your Internal Program?

There are things you believe to be true. You build your life around that truth. If you later find out it wasn't true, you rearrange all the connected elements of your life and look for a new truth to build upon. Once you have a new truth installed in your life, you live according to it.

They say the truth shall set you free. This infers that lies can bind you. How? When you believe something, you bind yourself to it. You hold on to it tightly. If it really is true, then you're fine. But if it is false, yet you perceive it as true, you don't want to let it go. To others it may seem like a lie has a hold on you, but truly you have a hold on it. Because you believe it is true.

Analyzing what you believe to determine how true it is, is a process that runs inside of you continually.

However, once you attach a religious or political "Truth" badge to some idea, you stop questioning it. You're no longer willing to challenge it.

This is why discussing religion and politics with a family member of a different persuasion at the family holiday dinner usually ends badly. Your family member is willing to challenge your assumptions when you are no longer willing to challenge them. You are now only willing to defend them.

It's alright, you were built this way. It's part of the human psyche to assign importance according to our values to different beliefs. Some you just believe, some you are willing to die for.

Every belief bears fruit. If the belief is bad, you may be believing a lie. Real truth will prove true and be quite reliable. You'll see the good that it brings over and again. But if you're holding onto a belief that is not true you'll be continually disappointed expecting one kind of fruit and getting another.

Finding truth is extremely important, you build your life upon what you perceive to be true. If it's not true you have a bad foundation.

The key to change is making sure that you have a foundation of truth. Making sure that the "truth" you're holding onto is really true. If you have "bad fruit" in your life, you are believing a lie somewhere. Sniff it out. Get it out! Once the lie is dislodged and replaced, the fruit you want can come forth.

Breaking the Stupid Lie

If you were told you were stupid then began to believe it, it would become lodged in your heart as a "Truth" (that was really a lie.) You would then align other things in your life with that belief.

"Stupid" is a demeaning term that speaks to how a person operates. It says that you make low quality decisions, that you have insufficient input, that wisdom is nowhere nearby when you decide something.

If you choose to accept that label, you are likely to assure that it is true. You will give yourself freedom to make dumb mistakes. You will even expect bad outcomes. You would never align yourself with a term like that if you had self-respect or had any inkling that you were worth something.

If that is you, consider doing this homework project: go ask a few friends to share three good qualities that they see in you. Write them down, or even better, record their voice saying them to you. Now, go read or listen to those over and again. Watch your response to what they say, are you rejecting what they say? Remember, you take what they say and pass it through your "truth" filter. These new statements will challenge the truth of your "truth". Hopefully you will begin to doubt the label "stupid". Doubting the "truths" in you that are bearing bad fruit is the key to removing them.

Maybe it's time to write down what you truly believe about yourself.

Now what kinds of edits would you like to make in what you wrote?

What if those good things they said about you were true? What could then be possible? How could you live if those things were true? What could you do?

Use this input to change your definition of you.

Once that definition is changed you can live at a whole new level.

Part 3

Sayings

Sayings

Sayings are interesting. Bundling a complete thought into a few words is almost sport.

King Solomon of the Old Testament, considered the wisest man, wrote a whole book of sayings, called Proverbs.

I've taken up this sport. I love thinking, observing, and writing. Hopefully these following sayings will bring some nuggets of useful wisdom to your life, hopefully, in the area of change.

Joe

Where Do Things Originate?

Happiness comes when someone chooses to celebrate the light instead of the darkness.

Disappointment comes when you are unhappily surprised by the outcome.

Happiness comes from the alignment of desires and happenings. Sometimes it takes work to get there, sometimes it's a gift.

Instability comes from 'knowing' something, but reality never seems to line up with it.

Freedom comes from being tied only to things that you desire. You're always tied to something.

Thinking

Of the making of many books there is no end...but then there is no end to man's need for what's in them.

"I Can't!"
...the signature of the one who signs his own death certificate or that of his dreams.

Dominion

Hunters load their guns when they go hunting. What preparations do you need to make to equip yourself to win today?

Strength is yours, act like it.

We are called to have dominion,
but not over each other.

When a king speaks, his motivation is to bring order into his kingdom. So, whatever is out of order in your life, be like a king, speak to it!

Write your plan for your future, if you do, you are being a good steward of your life.

See each area of your life as bank accounts – your responsibilities and relationships. Are you overdrawn in any of those accounts?

Those with a written plan for their life earn 10 times more than those who don't.

What do you want for your future?
Have you written it down as a goal?

Anger comes from knowing what is and what should be, there's a surge of motivation to change it. But don't lose control while you're angry.

Aim your anger at your problem but don't let your anger become a problem for someone else.

Rule yourself first. Expansion to larger boundaries comes if you manage yourself first.

Every action you take or don't, prove your dominion over your own self. Will you do what is right? Will you rule yourself wisely?

Be a great steward, you are in training to become a great owner.

The grip of jurisdiction an owner has released to a steward comes from the owner's trust of the steward. The owner will relax when the steward is faithful.

A high level of trust is in the heart of an owner who sees his steward loving what's under his care.

Caring about your jurisdiction, letting love flow from your heart toward that which you've been entrusted makes you great!

Goals

You've been given legs that are only so long. Whether short or long strides, many steps will be required to move forward. Goals must be broken down to the small steps required. No big steps ever really happen, they're all small steps.

When a group of people agree on a needed change, when they see the future the way it could be, they are the team who has the power. If they unify, communicate, imagine, and work then they are unstoppable.

Only you can see from your point of view.
Your opinion and your desires matter.
You have an appetite for positive change.
Get busy. Make it happen!

The things you don't like right now are the things you can change.
Define the goals.
Crush them.
Others around you then won't have to live in the same undesirable reality, the reality you despise.

Accomplishing goals, giving your time and energy to the changes you see fit, makes you an important and meaningful person.

Envision a future you desire.
Comparing now to that future will define what you still have to accomplish.
These are your goals.

What will you do after you achieve your goals? You can't know now; you will know then. Accomplishment will bring a new perspective… and new goals.

Things in the 'now' are broken, but they won't be in the future if you achieve your goals.

Goals are better than the current reality. Go ahead and change things to make those goals real!

Goals are you peeking into the future and deciding what should be, then you resolve to create that reality.

If you could throw an anchor into the future then use it to pull yourself to a specific location, that's what a goal is.

Focus

Your success depends on your focus, your focus depends on your self-control.

Teaching children to sit, focus and listen is essential to their academic success. As adults we should still practice this.

What you perceive fills you in some way. Pay more careful attention then to what is good and right. Fill yourself with what you want to have or become.

You choose where to look. Fill your eyes with light not darkness.

Desire helps to set and keep focus. Stare at what you want. Let desire increase. Your focus will follow your desire.

Incessant complainers need help.
They mainly focus on darkness.

Tell a complainer you love them. Many attempts at this may rescue them from their darkness. It will probably require many attempts.

Incessant complainers, although surrounded by problems, actually become the problem when they become addicted to the darkness.

Discipline

Discipline is needed where desire is depleted.

Nobody has to discipline themselves to eat ice cream.

Motivation must come from passion or discipline. Without one you need the other.

Discipline is a path to a change that must be.

Desire must be managed throughout the process. Continue to focus on the standard or change being acquired. Loss of focus will bring loss of progress.

Discipline expects momentum to kick in at some point. The highest intensity of discipline is needed to overcome inertia.

Once inertia begins to assist, it brings a note of accomplishment to encourage.

Discipline is knowing the path from where you are to where you want to be, executing it in spite of opposition or pain.

Hate is a strong word, but it is necessary to leave something behind. Severing ties must happen internally, you must hate what you must leave behind.

If the current state of being is acceptable then why change? Coming to the place of despising your current state is where you will begin to set goals and apply discipline.

If you accept yourself too much,
if you forgive yourself too much,
change won't happen.

Deep dissatisfaction with the current state of being strongly motivates toward discipline.

People seldom move before their pain threshold or tipping point is reached. Goals must be so strong that avoiding them is painful.

Your threshold of pain is a wonderful change catalyst. Are we there yet?

"Have to"
is a hard road.
"Want to"
is a delight.

Liking (or delighting in) the standard brings joy in conforming to it by:

- knowing the standard intimately,
- being familiar with it,
- being desirous, not jealous

will make taking on these characteristics easier.

Discipline aligns to a standard.
Habits cooperate with a standard.

Encouragement

Encouragement affirms worth, purpose, direction, and effort.

You are the ideal person to face this problem. You were born for this.

No one else is equipped the way you are to meet the difficulties in your life.
Victory is within reach.

You are sufficient,
but if you're not feeling it,
you can borrow someone else's sufficiency.
Ask for help.

Imagine that you are a bird, flying high above your problem.
Now look down on it.
Looks different huh?
That's a key to your victory.

You could tell 'em what's wrong or tell 'em what's right, one is criticism, one is encouragement. Which do you prefer?

Encouragement gives license to continue. Discouragement steals that license.

What would you like to tell yourself?

- write it down
- make a poster
- put it up on the wall
- say it out loud, you might listen to yourself.

The missing ingredient is often encouragement. Can you spare some?

What mighty works can happen when one stands by with encouragement freely given.

What mighty works can be stopped when one stands by with encouragement withheld.

Accomplishment comes when your effort and ability are greater than the need. That's a good way to live.

Sunrise is a daily hope-giving event. Take time to get filled up with it.

Give strength to the weak.
How do you do that?

- encourage with words
- help
- guidance
- money
- wisdom
- whatever is needed

Nobody thinks you're perfect,
you're not going to disappoint anyone by changing for the better.
Get to it.

To win you must be trying.

"Is there any room for me?"
Many ask that question and find no answer.
Encouraging words can guide people to their place.

Have you paid anyone a compliment lately?
What you say matters to others more than you know.

Leadership

What amazing things can be attained or accomplished when the masses are unified and led into action.
Leadership matters.

The inactivity of the masses is what leaders are sent to remedy.

When no one is moving, leaders will.
Leaders take the first step,
followers take the second.

Leaders have confidence in their cause,
followers have confidence in their leaders.

If you lead, you will be tested.
I hope you're up for it.
Someone needs you to pass the test.

Excuses are self-defense,
but they are at the same time self-defeating.
You can't hold on to excuses and win.

If you hold on tight to your excuses you will miss out on your potential. Everyone loses!

Thanksgiving

Can you think of anything to be thankful for?

Your focus determines the beauty you perceive.

A beautiful fragrant rose is never enjoyed without attention.

Being thankful helps you perceive beauty more frequently, more accurately.
Don't miss out!
Be thankful!

Take joy in creation by being thankful.

Happiness is a choice.
Thankfulness moves you toward it.
Complaining moves you away from it.

Expressing gratitude will make you a more appreciative person.

Being kind will make you a kinder person. Expressing anger will make you an angrier person. Do you want to be angrier or kinder?

You solidify your disposition with every action or expression of emotion.

Once you start being thankful you find more to be thankful about.

Habits use and create muscle memory.
Smiles are better than frowns.

Frowns and smiles both have muscle memory.
Smiling often makes it easier to smile often.

Smiles spoil a complainer's bad mood.
Rescue a complainer today.

Denial is when you are unwilling to believe you were that foolish and you don't want anyone else to believe it either.

Be skilled at giving thanks!
If you could earn a doctorate in Thanksgiving or Complaining, which would you choose?

A beautiful fragrant rose is never enjoyed without attention.
What are you missing out on?
Look around.
Give attention.
Enjoy!

Delighting in darkness will make your heart dark.
Abide in the light.

Giggling at other's pain does not make you a kinder person.

A small stone on the tracks can keep a large train from starting: a small negative comment at the beginning, can keep big things from happening.

Hearts thrive on affirmation not complaining. A thankful encourager is worth his weight in gold.

Thankfulness comes with the recognition of the good.

Nothing improves with constant complaining.

Sunshine and smiles can spoil a complainer's bad day, that's why most of them stay inside.

Final Thoughts

Friends, though this has not been a comprehensive look at the subject of change, I hope that I have served you with enough wisdom to get you thinking.

I endeavored to give you material you can use to affect change in your own life.

We are all on this battlefield.

We all must manage and wage our own war.

My hope is that you would know who you are created to be. That you do not throw away some of your true self just to become like another.

You are the only one with the recipe of you. You are truly needed in this world. And you becoming the best version of you is what this world really needs.

I believe you are "The Brave."

I believe you have the next steps to change.

You are on your way. Don't stop….

All the best to you, my friend!

Joe

More Information...

Prayer For New Life

If you could trade the life you've lived so far for the one God designed you for, would you do it?

If the Lord has been tugging at your heart to come closer to Him, it may be time to go ahead and give your whole life to Him.

If you've been weighed down with guilt and are tired of feeling ashamed and disgusted with how things have been going, it may be time! Time to finally say "yes" to a relationship, a real relationship with God.

He made a way for you to come to Him. He cleared a path. Jesus gave His life to cleanse you from all your sins and make you brand new. Are you ready?

The Bible says, when you call on the name of the Lord you will be saved. (Romans 10:13) Saved from what? Many things. The mess you're in, the future mess you're headed towards, especially Hell.

Give your life to Jesus and everything will become new for you. (2 Corinthians 5:17)

If you desire to have this new life in Christ, pray this now:

Heavenly Father,
I need you. I come to you as a sinner, needing a new life.
Forgive me of my sins. Make me brand new.
Give me a new life. Lord, I believe that you raised Jesus from the dead. Jesus, you are my Lord.
From this day on, God, I belong to you. My whole life is yours.
Let's live it together. In Jesus' name, Amen!

Prayer For Power

It seems that Jesus had more power to live victorious than we Christians do. He always had the right answer that blew everybody away. He didn't seem to need to obey natural laws. He walked on water, raised the dead, healed the sick, and fed multitudes with a little boy's lunch.

Are we supposed to imitate Him? Aren't we supposed to try to be like Him? It seems foolish. It's kind of like a kid with a Superman cape that wants to jump off the roof of the garage. It's cute but definitely not effective.

There is a different way. Jesus said in Acts 1:8, you would receive power when the Holy Spirit comes upon you. In 1 Corinthians 12, it says the Holy Spirit gives us gifts that are beyond human ability. In John chapters 14-16 Jesus introduces us to the ministry of the Holy Spirit through the most unlikely candidates– you and me! In the Book of Acts, the Holy Spirit came upon people who were praying. He came upon people when the disciples laid hands on them, but Jesus also promised that God would give the Holy Spirit to those who ask. Are you ready to ask? The only prerequisite is that you are a believer in Jesus Christ.

If you want to have power through the Holy Spirit, pray this now:

Heavenly Father,
I do believe in your Son, Jesus Christ. Jesus is my Lord. I want the same power that Jesus had so that I can imitate Him and live this life as He did. Lord, I ask you to fill me with your Holy Spirit right now. Holy Spirit, you are welcome in my life. Teach me. Lead me. Draw me closer and closer to God. Lord, use me to do whatever you want to do. In Jesus' name,
Amen!

Joseph Barlow

As the 10th of 14 children, Joe was born into a family that believed in training leaders and changing the world. Joe received his degree in Music Theory and Composition, after which he married his lovely wife, Nancy. Joe & Nancy have been married since 1985 and enjoy seven children and their families.

Being led by the Holy Spirit is the essential element of Joe's ministry and daily life. The focus of Joe's life is to draw people to God.

His extensive business background has brought great strength to his ministry calling. Joe has literally been involved in the ministry since he was 11. Pastored for 16 years and a worship leader for over 30. He served as the Director of Living Word School of Ministry in Forest Park.

He now runs Joseph Barlow Ministries where he focuses on teaching, writing books, writing and performing music, coaching, creating on-line classes, and ministry through social media and podcasts.

His 20 plus years of corporate work include management for Tyndale House Publishers, Christianity Today, database programming, being a Microsoft Certified Trainer and the Chief Operating Officer of a $550 million hedge fund.

The Barlow family are making their mark in the world as well - doing powerful things that we're sure you'll hear about in the future. (Isaiah 61:9)

Joe also has a side hustle playing guitar in various venues with his 60s and 70s hits.

Other titles by Joseph Barlow include:

- Prayer Is…
- Change Is For The Brave
- Texting Through The Clouds

Please consider joining the host of partners who are helping Joe reach so many with this ministry. www.josephbarlow.com/partner

For updated information about Joe's other products, meetings, coaching, streaming music, classes, travel schedule, podcasts, and much more please visit www.josephbarlow.com.

Made in the USA
Monee, IL
20 November 2023

46869296R10075